THE 8 STRATEGIES for ASPIRING LEADERS
Workbook

For licensing or permissions please contact
Black Belt Mindset Productions at 800-786-8502.

Contents

"The genuine leader is one who has the ability to attract WILLING followers—and the will to serve them."

About your workshop:

A message from Jim:

I encourage FULL CONTACT participation at my workshops!

If you have a question or comment at any time, please raise your hand, jump up and down- do anything (within reason!) to get my attention and I'll welcome your input!

If your workshop has live polling, please have your smartphone on and logged in. Login information will be provided on the presentation screen prior to your event.

There are no hypothetical exercises at my workshops. Be prepared to share real life experiences and challenges as we move through the program. Let's work on what's really happening in your life and business and send you home with ideas you can use—

Today!

About Jim:

Jim Bouchard transformed himself through martial arts from dropout, drug abuser and failure to successful entrepreneur & Black Belt.

As a speaker and author of **THE SENSEI LEADER** and **THINK Like a BLACK BELT** Jim tours nationally presenting his philosophy for corporate and conference audiences. He's a regular guest on TV and radio programs including **FOX News, BBC Worldview** and **FOX Across America.**

"People follow examples much more enthusiastically than they do orders—Lead by example!"

The Essential Characteristics of the SENSEI LEADER

"Wisdom, compassion, and courage are the three universally recognized moral qualities of men."

~ Confucius

From **THE SENSEI LEADER:**

I did not know this quotation when I started looking for the most essential qualities of an effective leader. I arrived at the same three qualities by asking kids what they were looking for in a leader.

That's right—kids!

For about 3 years I did an exercise with Junior Instructor trainees in my martial arts program. I asked them to come up with three words to describe a leader; someone they would follow willingly.

They came up with the same three words Confucius preached so long, long ago. No matter what age, what occupation or what demographic category, most people identify the same qualities these kids did year after year:

- *Courage*
- *Compassion*
- *Wisdom*

You can certainly add to the list, but limiting the list forces us to identify the most essential qualities—those qualities without which you simply cannot consider yourself an authentic or effective leader. Every other suggestion I've ever heard fits into one of these three buckets.

It's simple. Commit yourself to continual development and cultivation in these three areas and you will become a more effective and capable leader. Commit yourself to helping others develop these characteristics, and your power and effectiveness as a leader expands exponentially.

~

COURAGE

The **SENSEI LEADER 15** is a short set of 15 questions crafted to assess your strengths and areas for improvement in regard to the **Essential Qualities of an Effective Leader.**

The first 5 focus on **Courage.** Let's get started …

A1 There is no growth without risk.

	Strongly Agree
	Agree
	Disagree
	Strongly Disagree

A2 Challenges and obstacles are the best ways to test my talents, skills and abilities.

	Strongly Agree
	Agree
	Disagree
	Strongly Disagree

A3 It takes genuine courage to be creative and innovative.

	Strongly Agree
	Agree
	Not necessarily
	Disagree
	Strongly Disagree

A4 Doing the right thing is always the most important consideration, even when it's not profitable, expedient, popular or comfortable.

	Strongly Agree
	Agree
	There are exceptions to the rule
	Disagree
	Strongly Disagree

A5 Which of these statements best defines courage?

	Complete absence of fear
	Ability to manage fear
	Ability to act despite fear
	Ability to hide fear from others

You'll find a detailed discussion of these answers and what each *might* mean in the back of this workbook—but don't cheat!

For now, I'm just trying to instigate some thought and discussion.

Let's talk about your responses …

3

From **THE SENSEI LEADER:**

Courage is not the absence of fear. The absence of fear is stupidity.

General George S. Patton said;

"If we take the generally accepted definition of bravery as a quality which knows no fear, I have never seen a brave man. All men are frightened. The more intelligent they are, the more they are frightened."

Everyone, especially rational people, experience fear. It's natural. Fear is part of our survival mechanism. Fear is what separates the brave from the foolish.

Without fear, there is no courage. Any idiot can charge into trouble ignorant of danger. Courage is defined by your awareness of the risk involved.

Courage is your ability to face your fear and do what needs to be done in spite of it.

Of all the qualities of an effective leader, courage is the most iconic, and people expect you to have it.

Most of the time, people will forgive your mistakes and transgressions, sometimes to a surprising degree. They'll often overlook shortcomings, lack of knowledge, incompetence and sometimes even deception—

... but they'll never follow a coward.

It's part of your role as a leader to cultivate and express the characteristic of Courage. You practice and express courage by facing your fears.

Maybe even more important, it's your role to develop, support and *encourage* others. While you can only be courageous by facing your fears, you can give others the opportunity to express courage by mitigating their fears.

What are your greatest fears?

What are you doing to cultivate your own courage? How are you expanding your capability to act courageously?

What meaningful risks have you taken lately?

What are you doing to support your followers and embolden them to act courageously?

"You grow as a leader, and as a person, in direct proportion to what you're willing to share with others. You bring out the best in others not because you expect anything from them, but because you're willing to extend your best self first."

~Jim Bouchard

COMPASSION

The next 5 questions from the **SENSEI LEADER 15** focus on **Compassion.**

Don't think about your answers too much! There are no "right or wrong" answers, and your gut level response will generally be most accurate.

B1 I am comfortable expressing my feelings frankly with others.

	Always
	Usually
	Sometimes
	Never

B2 Before making an important decision, it is important to solicit input from key players at all levels.

	Strongly Agree
	Agree
	Disagree
	Strongly Disagree

B3 How often you openly recognize a co-worker or subordinate for a job well-done?

	Never
	Rarely
	Sometimes
	Frequently (Daily)

B4 I get as much satisfaction from the success of others than I do from my own achievements.

	Strongly Agree
	Agree
	About the same
	Disagree
	Strongly Disagree

B5 How well do you know your co-workers and subordinates?

	I know each of them personally and I know what motivates and inspires each of them.
	I know each of them very well professionally, but I do not get into personal lives.
	I know some very well, others not as much.
	I know little about any of them outside of roles on the job.

From **THE SENSEI LEADER:**

People want leaders who care about them.

People respond much better, work harder, produce more and create more new ideas when they know their leaders care.

When people have faith in leadership, they're more ambitious, courageous and innovative. They're more loyal, vested and committed.

The Sensei Leader practices caring in the form of sincere compassion and empathy. It's leadership on a personal level- an intimate level. This is exactly what people all over the world want and need from their leaders; and it's nothing new.

Compassion is not weakness. Genuine compassion is an expression of strength ...

Compassion goes much deeper than just being kind.

Compassion is genuine empathy; a sincere, mindful attempt to understand the feelings, needs and desires of others. If you want to be an effective leader, compassion involves developing a meaningful and authentic connection with the needs, desires and motivations of your followers.

WISDOM

The final 5 questions from the **SENSEI LEADER 15** focus on **Wisdom:**

"Now we're talking about the wisdom of the leader. Wisdom is knowledge and experience tempered by awareness." ~The Sensei Leader

C1 I am usually well aware of how my words and actions will be perceived by the people around me.

	Yes, usually.
	I am, but I'm sometimes surprised by the reaction of others.
	Sometimes people take my words and actions the wrong way.
	People just don't get me.

C2 When is it appropriate, more efficient or prudent to relax your efforts in personal or professional development?

	Once you've reached your goal
	Once you're "successful"
	As you're approaching your goal
	Never

C3 Personal development and professional development are inseparable.

	Strongly Agree
	Agree
	Disagree
	Strongly Disagree

C4 How important is emotional intelligence and inter-personal skill compared with the importance of intellectual intelligence, procedural knowledge and specific functional skills?

	"Hard" procedural skills, intellect are far more important.
	They are all equally important .
	Emotional intelligence and "soft" or interpersonal skills are most important.

C5 Ideas and vision must always flow from the top down.

	Strongly Agree
	Agree
	Disagree
	Strongly Disagree

"Management is efficiency in climbing the ladder of success—

leadership determines whether the ladder is leaning against the right wall."

~Stephen Covey

From **THE SENSEI LEADER:**

A leader can't rely on book smarts. You need to develop a deeper process; the ability to transform knowledge into something much more meaningful, something that can be expressed and shared and can transform lives.

That something is wisdom.

You develop wisdom by taking what you know and doing something with it. This means seeking out new challenges and new adventures—new opportunities to apply your knowledge to produce ever more powerful results.

Knowledge can be acquired. Wisdom is earned.

What are you currently doing to expand your wisdom, personally and professionally?

What are you doing to help others develop authentic wisdom?

"Study strategy over the years and achieve the spirit of the warrior. Today is victory over yourself of yesterday; tomorrow is your victory over lesser men."

~Miyamoto Musashi

8 STRATEGIES for ASPIRING LEADERS

8 STRATEGIES for ASPIRING LEADERS builds on the original **8 STRATEGIES for EFFECTIVE LEADERS** contained in **THE SENSEI LEADER.** Some of these are the same, but I've added a few others that will help you as you develop and

I believe Musashi would recognize some of them ...

#1 Work first on being a good follower
Great leaders are usually also good followers.

#2 Find the right Master
Finding the right teachers, coaches and mentors is one of the most important parts of your development as a leader.

#3 Commit yourself to personal and professional Mastery
If you're a leader, people expect you to know what you're doing!

#4 Ask before you're asked—Act before you're asked
Leaders lead and many times that means being first.

#5 Learn to deal with uncertainty
If you're going to be an effective leader, you'd best get comfortable with it!

#6 Learn to talk and write good
I hope you get the joke!

#7 Focus on experience over rewards
You deserve nothing—until you prove your actual value—through performance.

#8 Lead by sharing, not accumulating
You grow as a leader, and as a person, in direct proportion to what you're willing to share with others.

Let's discuss each strategy guided by these simple questions:

· **Are you utilizing each strategy effectively now? If so, how?**

· **How can you implement each strategy in your life and business—today?**

1) *Work first on being a good follower...*

Great leaders are usually also great followers.

1) How are you currently supporting the efforts of leaders on current projects and teams?

2) Identify a new opportunity to provide support to your current leadership.

3) If you currently hold a leadership role or position, identify one person who answers to you, and identify one specific way in which you could exchange roles to benefit team goals or objectives.

4) Who is the most effective "follower" you've ever known? What makes this person a good follower?

2) *Find the right Master...*

Finding the right teachers, mentors and coaches is one of the most important parts of your development as a leader—and as a person.

1) Do you currently have a mentor?

2) If not, what qualities or characteristics of a mentor are most important to you?

3) If you currently have a mentor, can you envision a time when you will "outgrow" your current mentor? What qualities do you need in your next mentor?

4) List 3 people you know who possess these qualities...

5) Are you willing to invest in a "professional" mentor or coach? If so, how much money and time are you willing to commit over the next year?

6) If you do not currently have a mentor, find one!

3) *Commit yourself to personal and professional Mastery ...*

Practice Mastery in your domain. At the same time acknowledge that you can't do everything yourself. Understand and cultivate the talents and skills of others to realize the full potential of the organization or community.

1) What are you doing right now to improve yourself professionally? Personally?

2) Identify 3 areas in which you would like to grow, advance or improve over the next year...

3) How can you best address each area? Class? Reading? Finding a mentor? Workshops? Other?

4) How much can you invest in your personal and professional growth right now materially, emotionally and spiritually?

5) If you can't "afford" the money or time, or you lack the drive, motivation, energy or support to focus on your own development right now, what steps can you take to increase your resources in any deficient area?

4) *Ask before you're asked—Act before you're asked...*

Most of all this means be first to do what needs to be done. While others are waiting around wondering who is going to make the first move, strap on your belt, roll up your sleeves and get to it.

1) Identify a specific need in your work or on your team that is not being currently addressed, or a specific action that can advance your team or organization...

2) Is there anything you can do on your own initiative to meet this need? If so, what can you do?

3) If you need approval, who should you approach with your idea?

4) Identify one action you can take on your own initiative—and do it!

5) *Learn to deal with uncertainty...*

Life is change, and for a leader, that reality is amplified by your responsibility to guide others through all this change and uncertainty.

1) Identify one area of uncertainty in your life or work...

2) Now identify one small step you can take to expose yourself to this uncertainty and address it...

3) Identify one activity or goal that interests you, but that you've been afraid to explore for any reason...

4) Do it! (Write down a date to start here—and stick to it!)

5) Do you know anyone else dealing with fear or anxiety over some uncertainty, change or danger? Can you help and if so, how?

6) *Learn to talk and write good...*

If you don't get the joke, we've got a lot of work to do!

1) Identify one area of communication in which you can improve your skills...

2) Identify one action step—class, workshop, self-study or group that will help you improve this skill—and do it! This could be anything from taking a writing class to joining a Toastmasters group...

3) Are you willing to share your development with others?

4) Identify a communication skill needing improvement in your organization. Prepare or organize training in that area...

5) Are you up to date on current communication platforms and their applications?

6) If not, what can you do to help yourself and others get current?

7) *Focus on experience over rewards...*

You "deserve" nothing—until you prove your actual value—through performance.

1) In your current position today, what do you really deserve? Are you getting it?

2) What have you done lately to justify your *current* value or compensation?

3) Identify 3 specific areas where you could increase your value to your team or organization over the next year...

4) Identify 3 specific experiences you've had in your role over the past year that have contributed value to your life or career...

5) How will these experiences benefit you in the future?

8) *Lead by sharing, not by accumulating.*

You grow as a leader, and as a person, in direct proportion to what you're willing to share with others.

1) Right now, what can you share and what are you willing to share with the people you live and work with?

2) If you are currently in a leadership role, what responsibilities, power and authority are you willing to share with others?

3) Identify 3 people you can share responsibility, power and authority with and specifically what you can share today...

4) Identify any areas in which you are not willing, or may be uncomfortable sharing with others and state why...

5) What can you do to make yourself more comfortable sharing in these areas?

"Be like water making its way through cracks. Do not be assertive, but adjust to the object, and you shall find a way around or through it. If nothing within you stays rigid, outward things will disclose themselves.

"Empty your mind, be formless. Shapeless, like water. If you put water into a cup, it becomes the cup. You put water into a bottle and it becomes the bottle. You put it in a teapot, it becomes the teapot.

"Now, water can flow or it can crash—

Be water, my friend."

~Bruce Lee

Tactics

From **THE SENSEI LEADER:**

Tactics inform techniques.

Let's say I'm fighting an opponent much bigger and stronger than I am.

I always tell my students, you can't fight strength with strength. Don't believe the martial arts mythology- size and strength is a great advantage in a fight. If someone is bigger and stronger you've got to find a way to counter that advantage.

Oppositional tactics won't work in this situation. I can't fight an overwhelming force with direct force. I've got to apply the tactics of deflection, leverage or borrowing.

Within each of those tactics, there are any number of techniques available. However, if you apply techniques for force on force encounters to a situation that requires leverage tactics, they simply won't work. You've got to apply the techniques that best apply to the tactical opportunities in any given situation.

One of the great weaknesses of ineffective leadership is an unwillingness to adjust one's thinking—being close minded to change.

If you understand tactics, you are better able to choose the right technique for each situation and adapt your tactics and techniques for changing conditions.

Once again we're going to work in real time with some simple, but thought provoking questions...

- **Where and when is each tactic appropriate and effective?**

- **When have you applied the wrong tactic to a particular situation?**

- **Which tactic may have worked better?**

- **How can you apply more the more advanced tactics of deflection, leverage and borrowing where you may have previously applied opposition?**

"Great causes in human affairs call out the great in men. But true greatness is not in nor of the single self; it is of that larger personality, that shared and sharing life with others, in which, each giving of his best for their betterment, we are greater than ourselves..."

~General Joshua L. Chamberlain

Opposition...

When we talk about opposition, we're talking about pure force: *mano a mano.*

Force on force opposition is expensive—in battle or in business.

Still, there are times when direct opposition is the only, if not the most convenient, efficient or desirable option ...

What are you willing to defend at any expense?

What forces are you willing to oppose no matter how difficult, challenging or risky?

Deflection

More efficient and very often more effective than opposition is the tactic of deflection.

In *Tai Chi Secrets of the Ancient Masters,* Dr. Yang, Jwing-Ming translates one of the *Taiji Classics:*

"No matter if he uses enormous power to attack me, I use four ounces to lead him aside, deflecting his one thousand pounds."

This is a very useful idea when you find yourself in front of a steamroller, literally or metaphorically! Dr. Yang adds these thoughts:

"If you try to make a sudden, major change in the course of an incoming attack, you might get bowled over by the forward momentum. Even if you succeeded, you would need to expend considerable force."

How often do leaders oppose an oncoming force instead of using the much more efficient tactic of deflection?

How can you apply the tactic of deflection in a current leadership situation?

Leverage

In physics and fighting, leverage is using mechanical advantage to amplify input energy to produce an exponential increase in power.

In leadership, your lever is the mind and you're often looking for psychological rather than mechanical advantage.

Inspiration and motivation are good levers for a leader. Through inspiration, you can leverage the skills, talents and energies of many people to produce a far greater result than can be accomplished by any individual working alone.

Opposition and deflection are almost always responsive tactics- that is we most often employ those tactics in response to some immediate threat or attack.

Leverage, borrowing and harmony can be employed proactively.

Be on the lookout constantly for opportunities to apply leverage and these higher tactics to innovate, create new opportunities and expand the power of the people you serve.

How can you best utilize the talents and abilities of the people you serve?

Borrowing

The most difficult tactic to master is borrowing.

Here's an example from self-defense:

Instead of blocking, (opposition), you step inside the arc of a punch, intercepting the strike without diminishing or even deflecting it's power. Then, with expert timing and position, you turn your hips adding your power to energy you borrow from your attacker. You blend your power with his and …

… wham! He's flat on his back.

This type of technique requires expert balance, focus and timing. You've got to master control of combined forces, both yours and your attacker's.

Borrowing is the art of recognizing and exploiting opportunities to combine the energies of those around you, plus your own, to create an exponentially more powerful outcome. That can be really exciting to a leader!

How can you best align your energy or vision with that of others in your team or organization—right now?

Harmony

Harmony combines all the previous tactics. This is truly "going with the flow." You operate in a state of active awareness where you recognize threats and opportunities in the moment and respond effectively, efficiently and naturally.

Be careful though! We love to turn simple but profound bits of practical philosophy into useless t-shirt slogans and allegedly motivational posters. "Go with the flow" doesn't mean you're just cork drifting with the current. It's not an excuse for ignorance, laziness or complacency.

Going with the flow assumes Mastery ...

It means you've got the skill, experience and awareness to be in complete synergy with the conditions and forces in your space and with the minds and hearts of the people around you- both enemy and ally.

Harmony is only achieved through Mastery ...

What can you do right now to improve your skills in each of the 5 Tactics?

Leadership at ALL Levels

From **THE SENSEI LEADER:**

Titles, diplomas, ranks and certificates don't make a leader. Courage, compassion and wisdom do, at any level …

… at *all* levels.

A large part of the mindset "gap" in leadership is the tendency to think that only "leaders" can lead. It does not take formal study or a position of authority to be a leader. There are plenty of extremely knowledgeable people in positions of authority that couldn't lead a monkey to a banana raffle!

Leaders are those people who step up to do what needs to be done—whether it's on the front line or the corner office.

Two simple questions…

What are you doing to develop yourself as a leader?

Even as you develop—how are you sharing leadership with others?

"Enlightened leadership is spiritual if we understand spirituality not as some kind of religious dogma or ideology but as the domain of awareness where we experience values like truth, goodness, beauty, love and compassion, and also intuition, creativity, insight and focused attention."

~Deepak Chopra

The Spirit of the Leader

From **THE SENSEI LEADER:**

Leadership is a spiritual experience.

Leadership is a capacity. It's your potential to inspire, teach, motivate and care for others. You can only experience leadership through action— through your expression of courage, compassion and wisdom and through your interactions with the people who are willing to follow you.

If you want to find your true spirit, your true potential to make a difference in the world, then make a difference in the lives of the people around you.

Be the Sensei.

Be the leader.

The most powerful question in philosophy: WHY?

"Why?" focuses your mind directly on purpose. When you think about why you want to lead, you define the meaning behind your calling to leadership.

This is not a "one-off." Do this exercise from time to time:

Dedicate some quiet time for reflection and ask yourself this one simple, but powerful question …

Why do you want to be a leader?

Analyzing your SENSEI LEADER 15 score

We designed **The SL 15** to help you assess how closely your current thoughts and actions align with **The Essential Characteristics of The Sensei Leader:**

- **Courage**
- **Compassion**
- **Wisdom**

There are no "right or wrong" answers. The way you respond to each item and how these responses relate to one another give you an accurate reflection of your capability and potential in the most human aspects of leadership.

This key will give you a starting point to reflect on your performance and potential as a leader.

Consider your your responses and and our discussions as a starting point to create an action plan for addressing weaknesses and building strengths.

Section A - Courage

Item	Response	Score
A1 There is no growth without risk.	Strongly Agree	5
	Agree	4
	Disagree	1
	Strongly Disagree	0
A2 Challenges and obstacles are the best ways to test my talents, skills and abilities.	Strongly Agree	5
	Agree	4
	Disagree	2
	Strongly Disagree	0
A3 It takes genuine courage to be creative and innovative.	Strongly Agree	5
	Agree	4
	Not necessarily	2
	Disagree	1
	Disagree Strongly	0
A4 Doing the right thing is always the most important consideration, even when it's not profitable, expedient, popular or comfortable.	Strongly Agree	5
	Agree	4
	There are exceptions to the rule	2
	Disagree	1
	Disagree Strongly	0
A5 Which of these statements best defines courage?	Complete absence of fear	0
	Ability to manage fear	2
	Ability to act despite fear	5
	Ability to hide fear from others	1

Your section score: _____

Section B - Compassion

Item	Response	Score
B1 I am comfortable expressing my feelings frankly with others.	Always	5
	Usually	4
	Sometimes	2
	Never	0
B2 Before making an important decision, it is important to solicit input from key players at all levels.	Strongly Agree	5
	Agree	3
	Disagree	1
	Strongly Disagree	0
B3 How often you openly recognize a co-worker or subordinate for a job well-done?	Never	0
	Rarely	1
	Sometimes	3
	Frequently Daily	5
B4 I get as much satisfaction from the success of others than I do from my own achievements.	Strongly Agree	5
	Agree	4
	About the same	3
	Disagree	1
	Strongly Disagree	0
B5 How well do you know your co-workers and subordinates?	I know each of them personally...	5
	I know each of them very well professionally...	3
	I know some very well, others not as much	2
	I know little about any of them outside of roles on the job	1

Your section score: _____

Section C - Wisdom

Item	Response	Score
C1 I am usually well aware of how my words and actions will be perceived by the people around me.	Yes, usually	5
	I am, but I'm sometimes surprised by the reaction of others	4
	Sometimes people take my words and actions the wrong way	2
	People just don't get me	0
C2 When is it appropriate, more efficient or prudent to relax your efforts in personal or professional development?	Once you've reached your goal	2
	Once you're "successful"	1
	As you're approaching your goal	0
	Never	5
C3 Personal development and professional development are inseparable.	Strongly Agree	5
	Agree	4
	Disagree	1
	Strongly Disagree	0
C4 How important is emotional intelligence and inter-personal skill...	"Hard" procedural skills, intellect are far more important	1
	They are all equally important	4
	Emotional intelligence and "soft" or interpersonal skills are most important	5
C5 Ideas and vision must always flow from the top down.	Strongly Agree	0
	Agree	2
	Disagree	4
	Strongly Disagree	5

Your section score: _____

Your Score...

The score alone does not make a Sensei Leader!

Think about your response to each question. You may agree or disagree- but this will give you a starting point to assess your capacity to be a courageous, compassionate and wise leader!

SECTION	Score
A - Courage	
B- Compassion	
C- Wisdom	
TOTAL:	

Total Score	Section Score		
63 to 75	21 to 25	**Black Belt!**	You're a **SENSEI LEADER**- but remember, "Perfection is not a destination..."
42 to 62	14 to 20	Brown Belt	You're on the right track!
21 to 61	7 to 13	Green Belt	You've got potential.
Less than 21	Less than 7	White Belt	You've got serious work to do!

To book Jim Bouchard:

Alex Armstrong
Black Belt Mindset Productions
800-786-8502
alex@JimBouchard.org